THE TWELVE UNBREAKABLE PRINCIPLES OF PARENTING

THE TWELVE UNBREAKABLE PRINCIPLES OF PARENTING

ANN LANG O'CONNOR

PUBLICATIONS

THE TWELVE UNBREAKABLE PRINCIPLES OF PARENTING
by Ann Lang O'Connor

Edited by Marcia Broucek
Cover design by Tom A. Wright
Text Design and typesetting by Patricia Lynch

"Servant Song" by Donna Marie McGargill, copyright 1984 by OCP Publications. Reprinted by permission.

"These Days" by Charles Olson, from *The Collected Poems of Charles Olson: Excluding the* Maximus *Poems*, published 1987 and reprinted with the permission of The University of California Press.

Scripture quotations are from the *New Revised Standard Version Bible*, copyright © 1989 by the Division of Christian Education of the National Council of the Churches of Christ in the USA. Used by permission.

Published by ACTA Publications, 5559 W. Howard Street, Skokie, IL 60077 (800) 397-2282 www.actapublications.com

Library of Congress Number: 2006925716
ISBN 10: 0-87946-305-8
ISBN 13: 978-0-87946-305-2
Printed in the United States of America
Year: 15 14 13 12 10 9 8 7 6
Printing: 10 9 8 7 6 5 4 3 2

CONTENTS

For my greatest teachers—
my parents: Francis Lang and Ann McCloskey
and my children: Ryan, Ellie and Gina—
with love and gratitude

Taped to the wall next to my desk is a cartoon that I cut out from *The New Yorker* magazine many years ago. It is a drawing of a man standing on a stack of self-help books with a noose around his neck.

This is usually how I feel after reading one of these types of books: "There is *no way* I will ever manage to do all of the things that are recommended in that book. My family, my life, my career will *never* be as neat and orderly as that author promises."

I continue to have to learn—because I keep making the same mistake—that it is useless, even harmful, to compare myself and my life with that of another. Comparisons either cause pain that we do not have what another person has—or that our children are not like other people's children—or they cause arrogance for the same reasons. If I had a motto, this would be it: Never, never compare my life to that of someone else, especially with regard to parenting and family life. This is an area in which we all strive to do our best, though many of us feel we have no idea what we are doing and none of us is fully prepared.

We can, however, learn from one another, and that is my goal in writing this book. It started one summer at the rectory where I work. The staff had spent some time brainstorming ideas for a mission statement for our parish—one that would clearly state our beliefs as an urban Catholic parish and how we act in accordance with those beliefs. With it, we could more easily make decisions about what course to take, which causes to support, and where to put our human and financial resources. It would allow us to answer the question, "Does this fit our goals as a parish?" If yes, we would consider it; if not, we wouldn't.

Fast forward to late August, which is always a busy, stressful time for my family. For one thing, there are the expenses associated with going back to school: tuition, uniforms, new shoes, backpacks and lunch boxes, as well as endless school supplies. And, for me, the stress is multiplied by having to go out and buy all this stuff elbow-to-elbow with the thousands of other parents who also hadn't shopped early. Then there is the reality of getting back into a routine: up and out by 8:00 a.m., uniforms ironed, teeth brushed, lunches made, homework done, (is it library day?), permission slips signed, etc., etc., etc.

Stress in our family usually translates into arguing in loud voices about who gets to ride in the front seat, who gets the last scoop of ice cream, who pushed whom, who started it, whose turn it is to watch the kids while the other gets something done, whether the leaf from the dining room table is okay to use as a roller blade ramp.... Sometimes I wondered how in the world I ever got stuck with such a group.

In the middle of all this, I sat down late one evening to go through some photographs to send to a friend of mine whom I hadn't seen in years. She had never met my husband or my children, so it was important to find just the right photos to send. I wanted the one that truly captured this one's smile, that one's eyes, this one's sweet nature. As it turned out, it was a very enjoyable task. I got lost in the process and browsed for a long time. As I was looking through these photos (and silently thanking my husband for taking them), I was reminded that there *were* happy times in our family—which being in the middle of a rather long stretch of feuding, I had quite forgotten.

A moment later I was literally struck by the idea that we are just five imperfect people trying to make a family. Looking at the faces in those photos, I realized that we are all human beings with different personalities, needs, wants, talents, desires, gifts, missions, paths, histories and futures. For the first time I understood that arguing and not getting along are inevitable in such an arrangement and, furthermore, that God wants us to work out this unwieldy thing called life—and to do it *together*.

Later I realized that all the different people, ministries, agendas, needs, wants and desires of our parish were not unlike those of my family. And that if—like the parish—I wanted to know where I was heading, if I wanted to feel confident that I was doing a reasonably good job at what I considered to be the single most important thing I would ever do, and if I wanted to create the wondrous, magical, happy childhood for my children that I had myself, then—like the parish—I had to write a mission statement.

Eventually my mission statement evolved into twelve core principles. I determined that out of the thousands of things I could choose to focus on as a parent these were the principles on which I wanted to center my energy and attention, so I could let go of all the rest without regret.

These twelve principles are a reflection of what I regard as important, based upon my own childhood experiences, my current interests, and the ways I want to act as a counterforce to the contemporary western culture in which we live. I don't claim to know more than anyone who reads this book, but I can say that I have given my role as a parent a lot of thought—mainly because I have found it so difficult and have felt lost so often.

I have written this book in the spirit of a poem by Charles Olson that I saw years ago on a city bus, of all places:

> whatever you have to say, leave
> the roots on, let them
> dangle
>
> And the dirt
>
> Just to make clear
> where they come from

These principles are the roots of what I have to say. They attempt to answer the questions "How did I decide on this?" and "Why is this important?" rather than "How do I do this?" because my experience has been that once I know *why*, the *how* generally takes care of itself.

I would feel a fraud if I didn't admit that I am not always able to follow my own principles. However, before I had a purpose but no direction; now I have both. Before I felt out of control; now I feel in control. Before I had no systematic way of making decisions about when to say yes to my children's relentless requests; now I do. (Let's see…is buying [name of desired item] on this list? No.) Before I hoped and prayed that my children would grow up to be happy, spiritual, contributing members of society; now I still hope and pray, but I also know that no matter what happens I will have done my best and will have done it consciously.

In the end, isn't that what we all want to be able to say?

1
THE ACCEPTANCE PRINCIPLE

Love and accept your children as they are.

Each one of us has a fundamental need to be accepted for who we are, and that includes our whole self: our faults and foibles, talents and strengths. When children feel fully accepted by another human being, they develop the enthusiasm and the will to learn, grow and flourish; to love themselves and others; and to accept responsibility for their actions.

We know this. The greater difficulty is to figure out *how* to love and accept our children. Clearly, there are many barriers to overcome, many misunderstandings that get in the way of truly loving our children as they are. To begin with, the word *love* has taken on so many different meanings and carries so much baggage that it is nearly useless as a concept. We love a certain food, we love our jobs, we are supposed to love our neighbor, we love the pair of shoes we saw in the store window, we love our families. All are common uses of the word love, yet all have different connotations and implications. It is helpful, then, to begin with a definition: *We love our children to the extent to which we accept them as they are.* In other words, love *is* accepting our children as they are.

Acceptance of our children as they are involves our will and must be a conscious, intentional and deliberate decision. This is especially true with a child who is always causing trouble, or who demands too much attention, or who is otherwise a challenge to live with and raise. Where do you draw the line between acceptance and being a doormat? If we can't stand their hairstyle or their messy room, does that mean we do not accept them? How do we influence our children and at the same time accept who they are? How do we avoid regularly becoming angry and impatient with our children for being works in progress? Finally, how do we accept the child who challenges all of our cherished notions of how a family should be, and in particular such things as how we spend our time together, what we buy with our money, and how children should behave toward their parents?

I have struggled with all of these questions at one time or another, and while I know that they will never be resolved once and for all,

I have found four strategies to be particularly helpful: *reconsider the Golden Rule; set aside your expectations; develop your neutrality;* and *know yourself.*

Reconsider the Golden Rule.

For a long time, whenever I had to leave the house for a meeting or to run an errand, one of my children would scream, cry, grab my legs, and wail, "Don't go; don't go!" My reaction to this melodramatic behavior was to wait until the very last minute to tell her I was going out. Somehow I thought that would help, or at the very least, shorten my exit scenes, but things only got worse.

One day it struck me that what my daughter objected to was the *surprise,* not the fact that I was leaving the house. When she knows in advance what is going to happen, the way she does in school, she is able to handle transitions, such as my going out, much more easily. We began using a family calendar so that everyone would know beforehand who was doing what and when each week. The tantrums stopped.

As I reflected on the dramatic change in our daughter's behavior, I realized that the calendar on the refrigerator was nothing less than a way for her to receive love from my husband and me. When she has clear expectations, clear boundaries, clear everything, she feels protected and loved. It occurred to me that up until then I had largely and unconsciously depended on my knowledge of *myself* and *my* likes and dislikes to create the harmonious household I desired. (*I* like a clean house; why isn't everyone grateful for all the cleaning I do around here? *I* don't care that the gas tank is almost empty; why should anyone else? *I* don't want and will not use a microwave oven, so why should we buy one?)

As I thought further about this, I realized that, in a family at least, the Golden Rule—which we all know, have grown up with, and tried to live by and drill into our children—*that* Golden Rule does not always work. "Do unto others as you would have them do unto you" is effective in formal interactions with people. It works at school and in the office, at the post office or in the grocery store, but as a way to reach a child (or a spouse, for that matter), it often misses the mark. Unfortunately, because the Golden Rule is such a powerful and deep-seated concept, because it is so ingrained in our thinking, it is very difficult to notice when it does not work. We continue to follow the rule, using *our* likes and dislikes to determine how to act, all the while blaming the trouble it causes on the *other* person. We think, "I'm treating my child (or my husband or my best friend) the way *I* want to be treated, what's the matter with him?"

The Golden Rule in Matthew 7:12 is one of the directives Jesus gave us about how to treat other people. It's a good rule. However, he gave us an even broader definition of what it means to love: "I give you a new commandment, that you love one another. Just as I have loved you, you also should love one another" (John 13:34).

How did Jesus love others? He loved them exactly as they were. He loved the sinners and the tax collectors; he loved Zaccheus and the woman caught in adultery; he loved the Samaritan woman at the well; he loved his persecutors. He didn't try to change the people he encountered. He didn't give them what *he* wanted to give them; he gave them what *they* needed—love wrapped in acceptance—and that is what caused the transformation in every person he met.

Most of the time there is very little difference between how we receive love and how others receive love. Maybe that's why it takes so long to notice when the Golden Rule isn't working. None of us likes to be yelled at, so we try not to yell at others. None of us likes to be ridiculed or teased or hit or called a name, so we teach our children not to do this. Most of this we know and do intuitively.

What I am talking about is more subtle. It's a way of looking at the world and our relationships that changes our perspective on everything. When we ask, "How does this person receive love?" we remove ourselves from the center of the universe and think of the other first. We acknowledge that each of us is unique, that we each have different needs and desires, that our way is not the only way. Our efforts are then channeled away from managing and controlling behavior and situations (which is not very effective), to actively searching for the ways each person receives love and trying to respond in kind.

Set aside your expectations.
Expectations are often very subtle. They come disguised as hopes and dreams for our children, which are as natural to a parent as the desire to hold a newborn baby.

In my own case, for example, for years—since long before I was married—I dreamed of having musical children. I vividly imagined children who were drawn to musical instruments (piano, flute, cello, violin, trumpet, guitar—I wasn't picky), who wanted to learn and who never had to be pushed to practice. They would play often and joyfully with each other, I would sing along, and everything would be perfect.

So far, though, none of my children seem to be getting the idea. Despite spending a fair amount of money on various instruments and lessons, we remain a musically deficient family. This has been the source of a vague, low-grade disappointment for me. Once I identified the source though, I was obliged to acknowledge that my desire for musical children had its roots in a regret I have about my own childhood. I took piano and violin lessons on and off for a number of years, but I never got beyond the "still struggling to practice" stage. To this day, I lament the fact that as a child I was unwilling to submit to the discipline of learning a musical instrument. It then became clear to me that because this is *my* regret, I have no right to expect it to be resolved and fulfilled by my children. I cannot be disappointed that they don't pursue *my* dream. They are who they are, they have their own dreams and aspirations, and they will have their own regrets, which may or may not be the same as mine.

I have since promised myself to take piano lessons as soon as I am finished writing this book. I have been surprised to discover that, far from being difficult, it's a relief to accept responsibility for my own dreams and allow my children to have theirs.

I am certain that I have many more expectations that have yet to be uncovered, and that some will be harder to set aside than others. Some may have to do with career choices my children will make or who they choose for a spouse. Some may have to do with how they wear their hair, or what books they like to read, or how they spend their free time. Many of my expectations I will not be aware of until they are not met. In every case, however, I will have the opportunity to notice how my expectations can ruin relationships, and I can choose to set my expectations aside.

Develop your neutrality.
Each generation finds its own way of expressing itself, which is often puzzling and sometimes frightening to parents. In my own case, my children's behavior sometimes seems so outrageous that I can only conclude that no good will ever come of them and that I will be lucky if they stay out of jail! Some of the things they say and do I would never have *dreamed* of saying or doing to *my* mother—although in my more serene moments I can remember as a child hearing my mother saying the same thing to me.

The idea to develop my neutrality came to me by way of a Chinese folk story. This is how it goes:

Long ago near the frontier lived an old man. One day he discovered that his horse was missing. It was said that the horse was seen running outside the border of the country. His neighbors came to comfort him for his unfortunate loss.

But the old man was unexpectedly calm and said, "How do you know this is a bad thing? I am not sure."

One night the old man heard some noise of horses and got up to see what it was. To his surprise, he saw another beautiful horse as well as his own outside his window. It was clear that his horse had brought a companion home. Hearing the news, the neighbors all came to say congratulations on his good luck. At the greetings, however, the old man was very calm and thoughtful. He said, "It is true that I got a new horse for nothing, but how do you know this is a good thing? I am not sure."

Sometime later, the son of the old man was riding the horse, fell off, and seriously injured his leg. After the accident, the son was never able to walk freely again. The neighbors once more came to comfort the old man, but he said, "How do you know this is a bad thing? I am not sure."

A year later, many of the youth from the area were recruited to fight in a war, and most of them died. The son of the old man was excused from his obligation to fight because of his disability, so he escaped death.

I think about this story a lot; its obvious moral has had a significant impact on the way I now respond to life. What I try to do (when I remember) is not to judge people or events but to accept them as "what is." Labeling something as "bad" clouds my ability to respond to it effectively and well; labeling something as "good" makes me want to keep forever whatever that good thing is, which of course I cannot do. On the other hand, to accept something as "what is" clears my mind of fear, anger, or the desire to cling, and makes possible a far more helpful, effective response.

To take a neutral position toward my children and their behavior takes a lot of conscientiousness and practice, but I have found it to be the single most helpful attitude to have. For years, when one of my children said or did something that I judged to be "bad," my mind went immediately into a pattern of thought like a needle in the groove of a record that always ended with the same song of regret: "If I had only. . . [when he was two or three or six], he wouldn't be doing this now."

My reaction, driven by fear or guilt or anger at myself, was never effective. Eventually, I realized that while it may be true that my child's behavior is due to a lack in my parenting it is not helpful to respond from that perspective. I cannot change the past or keep punishing myself for it. What I can do is to accept what *is*—not knowing and not deciding whether it is a good thing or a bad thing, not judging my child or myself. The times I remember to do this, my response is immeasurably more effective and the situation diffuses beautifully.

Part of staying neutral is to stop criticizing my children, and this has been one of the hardest things for me to do. For some reason, I am afraid that if I do not point out all their mistakes and poor attitudes they will not know what they are doing is "wrong" and will keep on doing it. We only have to look at our own response to criticism to know that nothing could be further from the truth. What is needed is not condemnation, but modeling; not disapproval, but *to show them another way.*

Consider this story from the Gospels:

> Jesus...went away to the district of Tyre and Sidon. Just then a Canaanite woman from that region came out and started shouting, "Have mercy on me, Lord, Son of David; my daughter is tormented by a demon." But he did not answer her at all. And his disciples came and urged him, saying, "Send her away, for she keeps shouting after us." He answered, "I was sent only to the lost sheep of the house of Israel." But she came and knelt before him, saying, "Lord, help me." He answered, "It is not fair to take the children's food and throw it to the dogs." She said, "Yes, Lord, yet even the dogs eat the crumbs that fall from their masters' table." Then Jesus answered her, "Woman, great is your faith! Let it be done for you as you wish." And her daughter was healed instantly. (Matthew 15:21-28)

What I understand from this passage is not that Jesus temporarily lost his compassion but that he saw in this exchange with the Canaanite woman an opportunity for his disciples to hear how *they* sounded. Jesus accomplished this by at first responding to the woman in the way he knew his disciples would have done: scornful of her pestering. Then he responded in his own compassionate way. He did not criticize his followers; he did not tell them how petty and small they were. He simply allowed them to hear themselves and then *showed them another way.*

A powerful contemporary version of this idea is one I heard on a National Public Radio show called *This American Life.* A father and his teenaged son were taking turns telling their story, which began with the son using and selling illegal drugs. When the father became aware of his son's activities, rather than confronting his son outright, he tapped the phone to record his son's drug deals. After some time, the father simply handed his son the tapes and asked him to listen to them. The son was so appalled by how stupid and awful he sounded on the tapes that he gave up dealing and using drugs altogether.

When I have the presence of mind to follow my own truth in this area (which I admit, and my children will confirm, is not nearly often enough), I am more effective and influential as a guiding force than at any other time.

As an aside, I have recently learned how grandparents, if you are lucky enough to have them around, can be invaluable for helping to develop neutrality. They have a long-term perspective and the emotional distance from their grandchildren that we parents do not have. Recently, I was grumbling to my mother about some aspect of my children's behavior. She looked at me and said, "*You* were exactly the same way—kids are like that!" My next thought was, "Oh. Well. I guess I didn't turn out so bad." I appreciated the reminder.

Know yourself.
One day I was poking around in the basement of the rectory where I work when I spotted a large brown paper bag full of books someone had donated. Not one to walk away from a pile of books, I went over to see what I might find. Sticking out of the bag was a small, yellowed

paperback called *A Guide for the Perplexed* by E. F. Schumacher. "Well, *I'm* perplexed," I thought, so I picked up the book and took it home. I began reading it that evening and could not put it down. It was one of those books I had been searching for my whole life.

Schumacher writes that in order to fulfill the purpose of our lives we must begin by striving to know ourselves. We must take that "journey into the interior," to use his words, so that we may become fully human and come to know just how rich, interesting and meaningful the world really is.

Self-knowledge is the foundation for understanding, loving and accepting other people. All of us are at times contradictory. We've all done things we're not proud of; we've all sinned. When we can recognize ourselves in another's actions, we go a long way toward being able to accept that person.

When someone does something that annoys me or makes me angry, I find it helpful to go within. There, in my heart of hearts, I am obliged to admit that I have done that too: I have procrastinated with work; I have not done what I said I would do; I have been difficult and unreasonable. When I recognize that I have done these things, it is very difficult to condemn the other person for doing the same thing. For me, anger toward or judgment of another person is a measure of how little I know myself. I keep at it.

Acceptance, however, does not mean that we allow our children to do anything they wish. Nor does it mean that we allow ourselves to become doormats. It *does* mean that we remember they are works in progress (as we all are), even when they are behaving like wild animals. Maturing is a long process called childhood, taking many years and much repetition. Parenting takes a mountain of patience and, above all, a *knowing* that our children will grow up well. I am convinced it's the knowing that creates the reality.

Fear, on the other hand, creates a different reality. Fear has its own energy, its own generativity, that—if sustained and acted upon—creates its own reality. It is fear that creates the feared outcome. It is acceptance of our children that creates acceptable children.

If I were a perfect parent, and loved and accepted my children as they are all the time, then it would be possible to stop writing here, because that's really all they need. But since I am far from perfect, I need more focus and direction. I need a lot more help. That's why there are eleven more principles.

2
THE GOD
PRINCIPLE

Help your children develop a rich and abiding relationship with God
by sharing your experiences of God
and encouraging them to share theirs.

I have not always known that each one of us has a relationship with God. As a child sitting in church, I didn't know it. For the two weeks each May that my family prayed the rosary on our knees in front of a large, rented statue of Mary in our living room, I didn't know it. During or after confession every Saturday afternoon, I didn't know it either. In every one of these situations and countless others like them, I remember trying very hard to feel something—holy, inspired, knowing—anything that would make me feel that I had the slightest connection to God, or at least that God knew I was alive. I never did.

And I might never have, were it not for my very perceptive younger sister. One afternoon she and I had gone to visit our father in the hospital where he was recovering from heart surgery. We had just left his room and were waiting for the elevator when I said stupidly, "Dad sure is lucky that he has such a wonderful relationship with God. I'm sure it will be a great source of comfort to him at this time."

Incredulous, my sister looked at me and said, "Lucky? He's been working at it his whole life!"

The unmistakable truth of her statement let loose a flash flood of memories that overwhelmed me for a moment, then receded, leaving the landscape of my belief and understanding transformed forever. During the few seconds between my sister's response and the opening of the elevator door, a vast and varied collection of memories of my father suddenly fit together and created a picture I had never noticed before.

I remembered my father and mother going to seven o'clock Mass every morning for the last thirty years. I pictured my father sitting in his favorite chair by the window, beads and wire in his lap, making rosaries to give away. Stacks of what we called his "holy books" lay on and under the table next to his favorite chair. These were the books that he read and re-read, the ones that must have provided much comfort and wisdom over the years. I recalled how every first Saturday of the month for as long as I could remember my father spent the day driving disabled adults to Mass for a group called The Apostolate of the Handicapped. I remembered what he told me many times: "When you are feeling sorry for yourself, go help someone else." This is how he lived, I realized; this is how he developed his palpable and profound relationship with God. The change in my understanding was as dramatic and obvious as a tree that has been uprooted by a flood and replanted somewhere else: My father didn't do these things because he had a relationship with God; he had a relationship with God because he did these things.

Along with these potent memories, what I had believed as a child returned to me. Some people (like my father) had a relationship with God, and others (like me) did not—the way some people have green eyes or a gift for music and others do not. It was simply the way things were, and there was not much that one could do about it. In those few, dense seconds with my sister, I realized with dismay that my beliefs about these things had never changed or developed as I grew older and that it had never once occurred to me to revisit them to see if they were still true. They had remained fixed for all these years at my ten-year-old level of understanding.

Standing there next to my sister, I experienced a deep feeling of regret for all the conversations I never had with my father about how to pray and why; whether he ever talked to God as a trusted friend or felt that God talked to him; if he ever felt close to God; what his image of God was and how it had changed over the years; how he experienced God each day and how he understood God working in his life.

My sister's remark ignited a fire inside me that apparently had been lying dormant all the years of my growing up. By the time we stepped out of the elevator, I had made two decisions: One was that I would find a way to work consciously on my relationship with God, and the other was that I would share my experiences of God with the children I hoped to have someday.

When my father recovered sufficiently from his surgery, I asked him what I should do to begin. He told me to go to church each Sunday and to ask God for help. The first part of his answer did not surprise me, but the second part did. It was a revelation and a relief to learn that

I could ask God to help me improve my relationship with God. I did what my father recommended, and these two steps set me on a path that has been the greatest source of peace I have ever known.

Two children later, I joined a women's spirituality group in our parish. Through reading and talking about good books; blessing pregnant women and, once the baby was born, bringing meals to the family; giving and receiving outgrown clothing and toys; and crying and laughing about life with young children, the women I met in that group taught me the supreme value of community and—most importantly for my spiritual growth—how to pray. I have since had many teachers, including a gifted artist friend who introduced me to Julia Cameron's book *The Artist's Way*. The fundamental principle of that book is that our buried creativity can be unearthed by writing three pages in long hand every morning. This discipline has turned out to be the most profound and satisfying method of prayer I have learned so far. The comfort and insight I have gained from writing what has evolved into a letter to God each morning is immeasurable and has helped me experience God as an integral, inseparable part of my life.

The decision to seek a relationship with God was the best one I ever made. I am convinced that our primary responsibility to our children is to convey to them that they are truly children of God and that their lives will be full to the extent that they develop this relationship.

It's tricky though. The "how to do this" has not automatically followed the "why it is important" in quite the way I hoped it would. Now I understand why my father never talked about this aspect of his life. It has occurred to me more than once to wonder whether I would have been interested if my father had tried to bring up the subject of God when I was a child. I doubt it. It is so very personal and difficult to verbalize. The ways I experience God working in my life are not always something that I feel I can, or even want to, share with my children.

My reluctance and—I'll name it—fear, combined with the nearly constant shortage of time and opportunity, work powerfully against conversations of this sort with my children. I've tried (sort of), but it's not possible to squeeze talk about God in between "Have you brushed your teeth?" and "I just washed that!" or, as they get older, "What do you mean you need a new red shirt for the music show tonight?"

Nevertheless, I am determined to find a way. Seeing the world through the eyes of a child helps. It is impossible not to be amazed at God's imagination and creativity when I look for signs of spring as though for the first time. How can I not marvel at the simple beauty and determined timeliness of the first crocus? The first blades of new grass? The budding of a tree? The brilliant colors of the first tulips and daffodils? The joyful noise of the returning birds?

For our children, naming the Creator of all is one way to begin. Pointing out to them the way God works in the events of our lives is another. Once I heard a story on the radio about a homeless man who was down to his last nickel, living without hope of finding a job or having much of a future of any sort. One day, as he described it, he "happened" to reach into his back pocket and found a pencil. He thought, "I don't have a job, but I can write something with this pencil." And he did. He wrote a book about his life as a homeless person. It had just been published, and this was why he was being interviewed on the radio. "That wasn't his idea; that was divine inspiration!" I exclaimed to whatever child was in the kitchen listening with me. I have often since used that story to illustrate for my children the way I understand how the spirit of God is at work in all aspects of our lives. I tell them that the more you notice God working in your life, the more there is to notice.

However, I am aware that this practice doesn't really get to the heart of "how" to help children develop their relationship with God. The traditional ways of communicating with God—church and prayer, to name two—do not always resonate with my children, as they did not with me when I was a child. Nearly every weekend my husband and I must contend with at least one child who does not want to go to church (which is why we need structure—I'll say more about that in the Structrure Principle), and I can't imagine getting them to pray *on their knees* the way I was expected to do as a child. Times have changed, and for better or worse, my children have no qualms about voicing (loudly) their objections to any such plan I might have.

In spite of themselves, though, I am convinced children need and want to pray, whether they admit it or not.

I have read that evening prayers are a good time to encourage children to talk to God, but bedtime is usually so raucous in our house that I can't wait for it to be over so I can go downstairs to wash the dishes. I once heard about a mother who blessed her children every morning before they left for school. This is a beautiful idea, but it's not my style. It would be awkward, and then I am sure my children would feel awkward too.

So far, the only regular prayer we've managed to incorporate into our daily schedule is at dinner time. Each evening, someone chooses a prayer to read from a book of meal blessings called *A Grateful Heart*. And while sometimes I have to bite my tongue to keep from expanding on the idea expressed within a given prayer (so as not to be perceived as lecturing), I am optimistic that the ideals of unity, gratitude and forgiveness, not to mention the value and variety of prayers, are somehow quietly lodging themselves in the hearts of my children.

I want to help them know they already have a relationship with God, but frankly I don't know quite how to do it. I do know that their relationship will be different than mine and will serve a different need and purpose. That is as it should be. Maybe it's an awareness will come in its own time, on its own terms, in its own way. I keep hoping that, until they ask me some direct questions, my serving as an example of a person of prayer will be enough. The rest I'll leave to God.

3
THE STRUCTURE PRINCIPLE

*Supply structure in your children's daily lives
by following a regular schedule for meals and bedtime,
family movie and game nights, and religious observances.*

Children—from birth to adolescence—need structure. They feel most secure when they know what to expect on a daily basis. They are happiest when, for example, their meals are ready at about the same time every day; they have a regular morning and evening routine; and their days have a pattern, a plan, and a relatively organized coming and going that they know about beforehand.

Children will never admit it, but they are counting on us to create this framework and to be consistent about upholding it for them. They will resist, they will whine, they will lean forward and swing their arms like a gorilla. But we can't listen to them. Inwardly, they are relying on us to supply the structure that they are not capable of supplying for themselves. Inwardly, they are hoping we will not give in—as they want to give in—to lethargy and inertia. Inwardly, they are depending on us to be the ones who maintain the rhythm, the flow, and especially the banks of the swirling, churning river rapids that they are.

Happily, this is one of those principles that resides at the intersection of a child's needs and those of a parent. We need the structure as much as our children do—not only for organizational purposes and sanity's sake but because daily, sometimes hourly, our children call upon us to make decisions about what, when, how, where, and with whom.

This unfortunate state of affairs stems from the fact that our children do not have the freedom that past generations of young people had. Gone are the days when children went outside in the morning and weren't seen or heard from until dinnertime. Instead, our children are at home, often inside, often depending on their caregiver for company because there aren't any other children on the block, or everybody is in daycare, or the parents don't know their neighbors, or the world is perceived as not a safe place. This lack of freedom for our children has lead to an over-dependence on parents for entertainment, companionship, transportation and money.

For instance, a little girl I know seems to spend most of her waking hours (and probably much of her sleep time) thinking of things to do that cost money, take up a lot of time, and/or require the company of an adult: "Can we see a movie today?" "Can we order a pizza and eat it in the living room?" "Can you take me to the store to buy a pair of overalls on the way to my Scout meeting?" "Can we go downtown after school, like around five o'clock, and ride our bikes along the lakefront?" "Can you drive me the two blocks to school, but stop at the store five blocks away to get a doughnut first?"

Unfortunately, if my information from other parents is correct, this child is not all that unusual. The frequency and complexity of her requests might be above average, but the difference is mainly one of degree, not form. The hard reality is that children ask their parents for a million things—sometimes all in one day.

Without the benefit of an established routine in a family, what often happens is one of two things: Either the parents end up doing everything the child asks for—which is very difficult (not to mention time consuming and expensive), or they say no a lot and are left feeling that whatever they *are* able to do for the child is not enough. Both situations result in considerable resentment on the part of the parents and the children.

In order to avoid this undesirable set of circumstances, I try first and foremost to remember that everyone has unmet wants and desires. As adults, however, we at least have the advantage of not having to depend on other people to get or do these things for us. This initial thought helps to stir and reinvigorate my compassion for my children, which in turn alleviates my tendency to be annoyed by their requests.

Second, I try to contain (in the sense of holding without judging) my children's unbridled yearnings.

Third, I try to remember that my children are counting on me to have the answer. And not just any answer: the same answer—time after time.

Finally, armed with a structure and a handful of predetermined responses, being compassionate and consistent is not as difficult as it sounds: "No, you can't [whatever it is], because we always play games on Tuesday nights" or "Today is Thursday; we are going to have pizza and rent a movie on Friday." Even more effective is to have a discussion beforehand in which we agree on certain things we will do, such as attend church every Sunday or how often we will go to a movie. Then we have an irrefutable response: "We already decided that, remember?"

By using this technique, before you know it you will have a whole stockpile of predetermined answers that you can pull out at a moment's notice. Here are a few examples of my favorite responses to the question "Why?"—which have the added advantage of being equally effective for "Why not?":

Because we *always* go to bed at 8:30 on school nights.

Because we *always* go to church on Sunday.

Because we *always* make our own thank you cards.

Because we *never* eat at fast-food restaurants.

Because we *never* buy video tapes; we rent them.

Because we *never* buy candy that is encased in plastic that will take ten thousand years to break down.

Because we *never* eat at any restaurant whose name is misspelled, such as "donuts" or "quik" or "cheez." (Actually, I've never used this one, but I'd like to!)

Knowing what my response is going to be before my child asks is like balm for my parental soul. It soothes and comforts, it provides courage and conviction, and it covers for a temporary lack of imagination or excess of grumpiness. At the same time, it is also true that there are days when it takes everything I have simply to maintain the routine. I am bored with the structure. I am tired of being the I-beam that holds up our family's life. I think I will scream if I repeat myself one more time.

What helps me hold up both the "vertical" and the "horizontal" aspects of family life is that I know that structure is important. And I know that its importance reaches beyond making decisions about what to do on any given day. It is crucial because routines evolve into traditions, and traditions identify who we are as a family. They also help mark time and, over the years, they become steeped in meaning and memory. These treasures demonstrate more clearly than we could ever convey with words the constancy, consistency, compassion and love we have for our children.

So, when you are tired of being the structure cop, keep this in mind: Few things will remain solidly in your child's memory beyond your family traditions. You have only to look at your own memories of your childhood to know that this is true. Be the one who upholds them. You will eventually be revered for your steadfastness. It will be one of the ways your child will be able to grasp the steadfastness of God. The Structure Principle truly is nothing less than that.

4
THE HOME
PRINCIPLE

Maintain an orderly home.

Notice that this principle doesn't say, "Maintain a *clean* home." There is a difference. While clean is good, I think it is less important than orderly, especially while children are young. At the heart of this principle is one important fact: It is impossible to maintain an orderly home if you or your children have too much stuff.

By "stuff" I mean anything that does not have a function or a purpose—like little plastic toys from fast-food restaurants and anything from a vending machine. "Stuff" includes all those things nobody ever looks at or uses but somehow you find yourself continually moving from place to place. "Stuff" doesn't even have beauty to recommend it. If you don't have a place for something or it doesn't have a function, give it away, recycle it, or as a last resort throw it out.

Better yet, don't buy it in the first place.

I became committed to this idea and found the determination to apply it from an exhibit at our local zoo, of all places. There, in between the elephants and the mountain goats, is a small but extraordinary exhibit devoted entirely to garbage. The exhibit's sole purpose is to make the very important and largely unacknowledged point that there is no such thing as throwing something away. We are able to maintain the illusion of getting rid of stuff only because we put it into a garbage can and after a few days somebody comes and takes it away—usually while we are not at home.

But garbage doesn't really go away. Ever. The plastic bags, the food packaging, the unwanted toy—not to mention two-year-old obsolete computers and exercise equipment—all are buried in the ground. Under the most favorable conditions, plastic takes ten thousand years to decompose. Unfortunately, our landfills do not provide the most favorable conditions. So most of what we put in there, for all practical purposes, is not going away.

When you buy something, *anything*, your purchase prompts someone in marketing to tell someone in manufacturing to make another one just like it. It is much easier just to say no when your children ask you for fifty cents to buy something from the vending machine or five dollars for some plastic do-dad from the discount store. Because ask they will.

Also implied in maintaining an orderly home is having a place for everything to reside. The key is to find or create a place where each thing belongs. This is where some imagination is called for. Even if it is a basket by the door or a wooden bowl on the kitchen counter, there needs to be a place for shoes and backpacks, gloves and hats and mittens, marbles and odd pieces to board games, and those cheap party favors your child can't bear to part with (yet).

While children will certainly benefit from living in an orderly home, I must acknowledge that this principle is primarily for the parent. This is because, in my experience, parents are the ones who suffer most when the home is not orderly. *We* can't go to work until our kindergartner finds her shoe. *We* have to stop what we are doing to find a mitten or an eraser or the library book that was due yesterday. I'm not sure why, but the children I know seem to be incapable of finding something if it is hidden—even only partially—under something else. Invariably, they will look over a room *without touching a thing* and say, "I can't find it!" Perhaps it is because the part of the brain that helps us find missing stuff doesn't fully develop until we are long out of the house with children of our own.

Whatever the case, one of our primary jobs as a parent is to create order out of chaos. We are the ones who must find a place for coats and hats, backpacks and books, keys and cards, stuffed animals and doll clothes. We are the ones responsible for having dishes washed and clean laundry in drawers. The children can and should help, but they are of assistance only if there is actually a place to put the things we are trying to organize. Otherwise, their idea of help is to move the stuff around from floor to table or from chair to staircase. But then *you* actually have to take it upstairs and find a place for it.

Organization and order seem to go against a child's natural tendency, which is to create disorder in a very short period of time. It helps to remember that order is a learned preference and that to teach our children anything—especially that which is in opposition to their nature—takes a lot of repetition and patience on our part, and a certain level of maturity on their part. In order not to become completely discouraged, I have come to see this aspect of parenting as sowing seeds, the fruits of which we may never see, much less taste.

Over the years I have learned to take my inspiration wherever I find it, and for this particularly thankless teaching job my guru is our school's band director. The first time I saw him was at a school Christmas concert. His students entered holding their instruments in what I presume was correct form. They bowed, sat down, and proceeded to play "Hot Cross Buns" as if it were the "Triumphal March" from *Aida*. It didn't sound like the "Triumphal March" of course (or very much like "Hot Cross Buns," for that matter), but the children played their parts with the reverence and concentration of seasoned musicians.

As I was listening, it struck me how many hours it must have taken each student simply to learn how to hold the instrument, produce a sound, read a note, and finally to do all three at the same time. How many hours of urging to practice on the part of the parents, how many hours of learning for each child—and the band collectively—that single, simple song represented.

The most amazing thing to me, however, was the band director's enthusiasm. He was completely delighted with his students' performance and obviously proud of their achievement. I thought, "Here is somebody who knows what 'Hot Cross Buns' is *supposed* to sound like, and yet he is completely delighted with these results!"

Here was a person, moreover, who most likely would never get to hear the fruits of his labor. As his students went on to high school and college, few would continue their musical education. Even fewer would go on to work as professional musicians. However, most of them undoubtedly developed some appreciation not only for music but also and especially for the value of hard work and practice. That is no small accomplishment.

If we could all be as enthusiastic as that band director, as grateful for small progress, as willing to simply sow seeds and not worry about the fruits that we may never see, the world would be a much better place.

I try to keep in mind that the level of order my children are willing and able to create is the physical equivalent of that performance of "Hot Cross Buns." It's not a symphony. But I look at it this way: If I work at developing my children's taste for order now, it's possible—even likely—that *their* families will enjoy the fruits of my labors. And somehow I think that having the gratitude of my sons- and daughters-in-law will be a very good thing. How's *that* for long-term thinking!

5
THE COMMUNITY PRINCIPLE

Give your children a strong sense of community
and a feeling of belonging
by participating in church, school and neighborhood events.

One morning I woke up thinking of a phrase from Rachel Carson's book *The Sense of Wonder* that I had read the night before. Here is what she wrote:

A child's world is fresh and new and beautiful, full of wonder and excitement. It is our misfortune that for most of us our clear-eyed vision, that true instinct for what is beautiful and awe-inspiring, is dimmed and even lost before we reach adulthood.

If I had influence with the good fairy who is supposed to preside over the christening of all children, I should ask that her gift to each child in the world be a sense of wonder so indestructible that it would last throughout life, as an unfailing antidote against the boredom and disenchantments of later years, the sterile preoccupation with things that are artificial, the alienation from the sources of our strength.

The last phrase is the one I woke up remembering: *"the sources of our strength."* It occurred to me that I had read these words many times before, without once thinking what they meant. What, exactly, *are* the sources of our strength? Are mine different from other people's? Are there some that are common to us all, just because we are human?

It's important to identify our sources of strength, because then we can draw on them intentionally and regularly, instead of accidentally and randomly. We can consciously use the sources of our strength to create peace, comfort and stability within ourselves, which will inevitably flow outward and benefit our families and others close to us.

Because we are unique individuals, each of us has unique sources of strength. For some it might be music or prayer or reading; for others, silence or exercise or a meaningful conversation. Do you know what yours is? It's worth reflecting upon.

At the same time, we are all human beings. Like every other human being who has ever lived, or is living now, or will live in the future, we have sources of strength in common. Two in particular come to mind: God, as expressed through creation, and community.

As the source of everything, God is our ultimate resource. Whether or not we have a conscious relationship with God, we all experience God's creation. Nature is always available to draw upon as a source of strength. For those of us who live at the far end of mass production, who do not see the enormous amount of processing and packaging and shipping between the cotton plant and the finished shirt, the tree and the wooden chair, the pineapple and the can of fruit cocktail, the miracles of nature can be more elusive. Still, each one of us is capable of appreciating the beauty and symmetry of a tree in winter, or delighting in a sunset, or feeling awe during a summer thunderstorm.

Our other common source of strength is community.

One evening during a particularly painful and lonely period of my life, I attended our parish play. As I entered the gym, I saw people standing around in groups laughing and talking. Children were running around excitedly, happy to be out past their bedtime, eager to see their mom or dad or grandmother on the stage. I felt the happy anticipation that always precedes an event like this. Looking around at all those familiar faces, I was overcome by gratitude for my church community—all these people working and loving and dreaming and planning.

That night the gym full of people and the whole parish appeared to me as a huge star, a sun generating and emitting the warmth and light that makes growth possible. I knew that I was a recipient of that life-giving energy. Although I felt wholly unworthy at the time, I allowed myself to absorb it and be strengthened by it. At the same time, I saw myself as a planet being kept in orbit by the gravity of this huge thing, and I knew that were it not for this parish, these people, this community, I might very well go spinning off alone into another galaxy.

Beyond our individual relationships stands the community as a whole, which simply by its size and weight has an influence and a pull that we are more or less aware of at different times in our lives. To feel part of such a community is a great gift, a deep source of strength and comfort, especially when we feel alienated from ourselves. When our children are part of a community, they will have a sense of place. They know they have come from somewhere. The community will give them strong roots that will serve them well as they grow up and move on.

I usually think of roots as primarily a stabilizing force: They keep the tree from falling over. But of course roots also provide nourishment. They are the way a plant receives sustenance. The deeper and wider the roots are, the greater the variety of nourishment. The same is true of the community: The more local experiences we and our children have, the more local people we come into contact with and get to know, the richer our lives and their childhood will be.

One example is the potluck suppers that our children's school organizes to help parents get to know each other. Invariably during the course of the conversation, someone brings up his or her own childhood experiences. No matter where they grew up, one thing that adults vividly remember is being yelled at by somebody else's mother. And people liked that. Even as children they liked that. I remember liking it too. It wasn't something we had to grow up to appreciate. We appreciated then it because embedded in the knowledge that somebody else's mother was looking out for us was a kernel of security that provided a deep sense of comfort along with the awareness that we were part of a larger human family.

At this point in the dinner conversation, someone always gives permission to the other parents at the table to yell at his or her kids if they see them doing something they're not supposed to be doing. Then, all the other parents give their permission too. That's the moment I always wait for. That's the moment when this group of people, most of whom did not know each other before they sat down, becomes connected through their children to each other. This is when parents recognize their dependence on one another, when they experience the profound truth of the proverb, "It takes a village to raise a child."

To know the people and the history of a place gives us a context for our lives. It implies that we have spent some time there, have gotten to know the people, have given ourselves over to something larger than ourselves. It puts us and our lives into proper perspective. We have a history, and it's part of a larger history; our life experience is rich and dense—it is "thick," in the sociological meaning of the term.

Finally, being part of a community provides a real sense of reverberation: When something happens to a member of the community, it happens to us all. And to know from lived experience that we are all connected is a very good thing indeed.

6
THE RESPONSIBILITY
PRINCIPLE

Teach your children to take responsibility for their own actions, their work, their school, and their neighborhood by holding them accountable and demonstrating that individuals matter.

If I could teach my children only one lesson, the Responsibility Principle would be it. I think it is so important because, for one thing, it's the truth. Whether or not we *accept* the responsibility, we *are* responsible. To accept responsibility means that we are both able (which implies self-awareness) and willing (which implies humility) to admit our mistakes, poor judgment, or whatever our shortcomings are.

Responsibility is important also because when we accept responsibility for our actions we keep the power to act or not to act where it belongs: with ourselves. Responsibility means that individuals matter, that what we do matters.

Unfortunately, personal responsibility is also one of the most difficult things to teach, partly because it has to be demonstrated over and over again—consistency is critical—and partly because the children I encounter don't want to learn it. (Many adults don't want to learn it either!) Why should they? It is so much easier to blame the other guy. But teach it we must, if we want our children to grow up with a healthy level of self-esteem balanced with a generous dose of humility.

Because it is so important to me, and because I have spent so much time thinking about it, this is the area where I have become aware of the most glaring contradictions in my parenting. This is where I am most likely to catch myself demonstrating the opposite of what I want my children to be and do.

The only way to hold my children accountable for their actions is to hold myself accountable for my actions, which also—and especially—includes my response to their actions. This takes constant vigilance. For example, as much as I would like to be able to continue saying, "*You* make me so angry!" or "I am grumpy because *you* are being rude and difficult!" I cannot. I cannot simultaneously hold my children responsible for *their* actions and, at the same time, make them responsible for *my* feelings.

When I finally accepted this truth, I understood that my children are my teachers and that I was the one who was being lead to a more authentic, honest self. Now, whenever I try to avoid taking responsibility for my own actions, I am likely to hear the tinny, clanging sound of hypocrisy in my voice. The dissonance is my signal to apologize and take responsibility. I try to be grateful for the lessons.

Beyond personal responsibility, the ways we try to teach our children responsibility for the larger community can be grouped under the heading: *"If I [you, we] don't, who will?"* In our family this question is both our motivation and our stock response to any and all complaints about giving money to the homeless person on the street, picking up garbage to and from school, volunteering at church or school, cooking for a sick person, helping out a new mother, or visiting a neighbor in the hospital. Because all of these activities take time and money and attention away from the family, our children raise objections from time to time, and all of them are overruled with this simple question: "If I [you, we] don't, who will?"

The second half of this principle, that "individuals matter," has to do with the power of the individual to effect change. I vividly remember a dinner conversation I had in the early eighties with two young, black South African labor leaders visiting the United States. Toward the end of the dinner, one of them asked me, "How do you think political change will occur in South Africa?"

To this day I don't know why he asked me that question. Given the little I knew about the situation there, I had no right even to hazard a guess. However, not to respond didn't seem an option. Mentally flipping through my college political history books, I couldn't recall a single instance of peaceful revolution, so the only thing I could think to say was, "Prolonged armed struggle."

I had not yet heard of F.W. de Klerk. (In 1990, South African President F.W. de Klerk made the dramatic decision to release South Africa leader Nelson Mandela from prison, where he had been held for the previous twenty-six years. De Klerk's action was the first major step in the peaceful dismantling of apartheid.)

The fact that I was so completely wrong about South Africa's future has kept that conversation in my memory all these years. Not because I cared that I was wrong, but because de Klerk demonstrated the power of a single individual with compassion and vision to change the world. What I had thought was impossible was not only possible, but actually occurred. Now I wonder, what else might be possible?

When I first wrote the Responsbility Principle, I wanted my children to understand that change can begin with a single person and that we all have the right, as well as the responsibility, to work toward a just society. I wanted my children to have the heart to hope and dream, to imagine and try.

However, as I have thought about this and tried to live it, what I want to convey has both broadened and deepened. "Individuals matter" has come to mean something much more than the idea that one person can make things better. "Individuals matter" has come to mean, for me, that we are literally all one body, that what we do to each other we do to ourselves, and that every encounter with another person is brimming with possibilities.

As I look back over my life, the image I see is a balance scale. On one side are heavy weights representing the objective experiences of my outer life, and on the other are tiny feathers representing my subjective, interior experiences. Over my lifetime, the feathers have gradually, almost imperceptibly, accumulated a weight and density that has tipped the scale of my worldview from doubt to faith, from belief in the visible to acceptance of the invisible, from concern for the measurable to delight in the immeasurable.

My first experiences with the imperceptible occurred very early in my childhood. I remember being told first by my parents and later by my teachers that I should "offer it up" whenever I whined about having to do homework or chores, eat my vegetables, or do anything I didn't want to do. The message was clear: By suffering without complaint and then "offering it up," I could help people halfway across the world. This was a very mysterious and wonderful idea to me. The thought that a prayer or a good deed could somehow ease the suffering of a starving child in Africa was a notion I could barely contain. It filled me with a wonder and awe that I still feel today.

This was the first feather on my scale.

When I was about nine or ten—that is, when I began to have both the opportunities and the power to act autonomously—the twenty-fifth chapter of the Gospel of Matthew attracted my attention:

> "Lord, when was it that we saw you hungry and gave you food, or thirsty and gave you something to drink? And when was it that we saw you a stranger and welcomed you, or naked and gave you clothing? And when was it that we saw you sick or in prison and visited you?" And the king will answer them, "Truly I tell you, just as you did it to one of the least of these who are members of my family, you did it to me." (Matthew 25:37-40)

On the way to the store or to school, in the park or at the library, I imagined that every stranger I passed or encountered was Jesus himself, and I tried to act accordingly. I was unfailingly polite, generous when I had the means to be, and always walked away wondering, "Was *that* Jesus? That might have been Jesus!"

Literalist that I was, it never occurred to me to extend the idea that *Jesus is in everyone* to include my friends and family. No, my best manners and generosity were usually reserved for strangers. In all other respects I was an ordinary child who fought with her siblings, lied on occasion, sometimes took the last scoop of ice cream, and vied for attention in school and at home.

After I had children, the story of the man born blind (John 9:1-7) became an important inspiration for me. Jesus' followers passed a man sitting by the side of the road, and they turned to ask Jesus, "Rabbi, who sinned, this man or his parents, that he was born blind?" Jesus responded, "Neither this man nor his parents sinned; he was born blind so that God's works might be revealed in him." As I understand this story, Jesus saw this man not as a problem to be solved but as an opportunity to demonstrate how love operates.

I have come to carry this idea with me: The person crossing my path is there so that I may demonstrate how love operates by how I respond. Whether it's with a homeless person on the street, the woman at the checkout counter in the supermarket, or my own child, every encounter becomes important and full of meaning. To approach life this way is to comprehend what Emily Dickinson meant when she wrote, "To live is so startling it leaves little time for anything else."

It is as simple and complex as that. To live with responsibility makes life rich and deep and interesting. It lifts our daily experiences out of the realm of the ordinary and into that of the extraordinary. It shines a spotlight on the invisible reality to which we are all connected in an incomprehensibly complex way. Physicists have a name for it. They call it "the butterfly effect." This is a simple but profound concept we can teach our children. When the wing of a butterfly is injured, the reverberations from the injury flow out like ripples in a pond throughout the entire universe. We can use this image to help our children grasp the idea that when one person is injured or, conversely, cared for, all of us are affected. The effect is very subtle, of course, which is why it is so often ignored—or not even perceived in the first place.

I know I have come late in life to this conscious, though still partial, understanding of the mystery of responsibility. I also know that is why I am not as consistent in my behavior toward my children as I would like to be. Still, I work at it. I keep hoping that a muted—even sometimes ambiguous—message is better than no message at all. I keep counting on the fact that accumulated experience will eventually compensate for inconsistency. And I keep praying that in spite of my fits and starts my children will grow up to grasp more fully than I the incredible implication of Jesus' statement, "Whatever you did for one of these least brothers of mine, you did for me." It would be so much easier to believe that this statement is simply a metaphor instead of something literally true, because that would require much less of our time and energy, imagination and kindness. But it is not nearly so awesome and inspiring. Nor, when you think about it, is it worthy of the God who created us.

7
THE EARTH
PRINCIPLE

Foster a reverence for nature
by helping your children notice the beauty that surrounds them
and teaching them to use the earth's resources in moderation.

One year on the evening of the summer solstice, June twenty-first, our family participated in a grassroots symbolic effort to promote energy conservation. People across the country created a "Roll Your Own Blackout" by unplugging all of the electrical devices in their homes for three hours that evening.

As we gathered around the coffee table to light some candles and tell stories, we were doing the usual negotiations about who was going to sit where, who had the most pillows, who got the red chair, whose blanket was touching whom, etc., etc., etc., when I noticed my son carefully taking our Shaker candle box down from its awkward spot on top of the encyclopedias on the bookshelf. I watched as he slowly opened the box and peered inside. With my mind's eye I looked into that box, too, and I could see what was in there: a hodgepodge of cheap paraffin candles from the grocery store that drip wax all over everything as the flame burns down the wick like a spark on a fuse.

Clouds of regret and missed opportunity gathered in my mind, and I wished fervently that the box had been filled with fine beeswax candles in pastel colors, each wrapped in tissue and carefully placed inside with a palpable measure of care and reverence. For if the box had been filled with beeswax candles, my son would surely have noticed their fragrance as he unwrapped each one. The distinctive scent of beeswax might then have become entwined with his memories of childhood, such that whenever he smelled it he would remember this house and the evenings we gathered together around this table.

He might have thought of the hundreds, perhaps thousands, of bees that made the wax. He might have recalled from the books we have read that bees secrete the wax from glands inside their bodies, and that they chew and shape it into perfect hexagonal cells, which mathematicians have studied and found to be the most efficient possible use of space.

He might have remembered that returning bees dance to show the other bees in the hive where to find flowers. The dance uses the position of the sun, like north on a compass, for orientation, so that the other bees can find the flowers with minimum time and effort.

His next thought might well have been of the flowers themselves. He might have imagined a perfect pink rose, or the hollyhocks growing along the fence in our backyard. He might have thought of the incredible variety and abundance of flowers, and especially of their beauty and fragrance. He would surely have remembered that it is actually possible to grow these magnificent blossoms with nothing more than a pot of soil, some water, light and a seed. Thinking of all these things, my son could not have failed to be amazed at the marvels of the universe and of God, its Creator. I was humbled when I imagined how much he might have learned without my saying a word, if only I had been better prepared.

Ever since that evening, I have sought ways to heighten my children's awareness of the wonder of nature without actually talking about it. We take walks at all hours and in all seasons along Lake Michigan. We collect rocks and beach glass. We press leaves and make leaf prints. We buy produce and flowers at the farmers' market. We watch raspberries grow in our backyard. We use beeswax candles.

My daughter's scout troop has been a good source for ideas. For example, during their campouts one group of girls is assigned to create a centerpiece for the table each day. They collect flowers, rocks, leaves, pinecones, seed pods—anything they find that they like—and using someone's wrinkly bandana as a base they create a centerpiece that is always beautiful, always evocative of the season and the place. At home, I use a piece of slate as a base (because it doesn't have to be washed or ironed). We always have a candle, a rock, and depending on the time of year some flowers or leaves or beach glass—anything that reminds us of the season or the events of the day. On someone's birthday we might add a photograph or two to the centerpiece, along with an object that reminds us of the birthday boy or girl. Often I have found that asking a bored and hungry child, who would otherwise be driving me crazy, to make a centerpiece for the dinner table is an effective way for a child to pass the time.

Once, for a combination scavenger/treasure hunt, each group of scouts was given a bag of supplies for the trail. One of these items was, simply and beautifully, an egg. Its sole purpose was to be cared for and returned unbroken as the girls followed clues, played games, solved riddles and performed tasks. Minding the egg turned out to be a coveted responsibility. One group went so far as to name their egg, and in the process they shared their experiences of death in that wonderfully matter-of-fact way children have. Their leader was practically in tears. (One way to incorporate this kind of awareness into everyday life might involve giving one or two beautiful, possibly old, objects to each child to care for and, hopefully, grow to cherish. But please don't choose anything that would upset you if it is lost or broken.)

Creation speaks for itself, but words and rituals can and do have the power to deepen our experience of it. On the occasion of the opening of the National Museum of Women in the Arts in Washington, D.C., co-founder Wilhelmina Holladay recalled how as a young child her grandmother took her for walks in the garden. Each time they stopped to look at something growing there, her grandmother would ask what it was that made the thing beautiful. Was it the color, the shape of the petals, the fragrance, or something else? Holladay attributed her lifelong love of art and awareness of beauty to those early conversations with her grandmother.

Whenever I take my children on a walk around the neighborhood to look for signs of the approaching season, I ask them the same question. I have found that as soon as we start thinking about what we like about something our powers of observation increase. I am aware, however, that I still have a long way to go. Once I needed to draw a squirrel for a class I was teaching. Try as I might, I could not remember if their ears were visible. I eventually had to ask my children. One said, "Yeah, they have ears. Remember in the [Disney] *Sword in the Stone* when Arthur and Merlin turn into squirrels? You can see their ears." Clearly, my children and I need to stop and observe and describe what we see around us more often!

It's one thing to foster a reverence for nature in our children. It's quite another to make the connection between our consumer lifestyle and world pollution, hunger and poverty. This came to my attention some years ago during a conference my children and I attended at a local university. During the three days we were there, we ate our meals in the cafeteria. Naturally, the kids loved this because they could serve themselves, choosing not only what to eat but also how much. I was appalled by how much food they put on their plates and especially by how much they threw away. You would have thought they hadn't had a decent meal in years.

It's not that I hadn't seen my children waste food before. This is a constant source of annoyance for my husband and me, and at home there is the added insult of seeing dollars going into the garbage can along with the unfinished sandwiches and the half-eaten apples. However, it was the *level* of wastefulness in the cafeteria that made me so indignant. I thought, "Don't these kids know how much time it takes to bake a loaf of bread? Not to mention how long it takes to plant wheat, tend it, water it, weed it, harvest it, grind it into flour? And how about the apple juice? Don't they realize that it takes years to grow an apple tree, and then a spring and a summer's worth of sunshine and rain to produce an apple that makes a quarter cup of juice?"

Just as I was about to ride off on my high horse into the sunset, leaving my children in a cloud of dust, I realized they didn't know all of this because they hadn't been taught it. And really, I asked myself, how could they possibly be expected to know these things when they are surrounded by abundance? When there is a refrigerator where unending quantities of food magically appear at least once a week? When there is never a sense of depletion because any time we are out of juice (or bread or milk) one of us goes to the store and buys more?

This insight led to more questions. How can our children internalize a reverence for nature that translates into an abhorrence for pollution and waste of all kinds? These are not easy questions to answer or to address. Poverty and hunger; pollution caused by power plants, factories and automobiles; garbage collecting in landfills—all of these are little more than abstractions to most children and to many adults. It's easy to understand why: In almost every case, we do not see or experience directly the consequences of our actions. The pollution from our cars disappears quickly. The power plant is miles away. So are the landfills. We don't know who made our clothing, or under what conditions. We have full plates, doesn't everybody? Even if we know that not everybody has a full plate, what can we do about it? How will eating everything on our plate help the situation?

Our family's response to the Earth Principle has been to recycle and compost, to walk to the grocery store instead of drive, to buy organic food when possible, to let the refrigerator become empty, to frequent yard sales and buy second-hand clothing—none of which seems enough. So we read books like *Small Is Beautiful* by E. F. Schumacher, *Food & Faith* and *Simpler Living, Compassionate Life* (both edited by Michael Schut), and anything by Wendell Berry. We talk with our children about economic justice, over-consumption, and how life is in other parts of the world. We keep hoping, even though our actions continue to fall short, that our will, desire and yearnings are enough to convey to our children a vision of a flourishing humanity on a thriving earth in an evolving universe, all suffused with the glory of God.

8
THE READING
PRINCIPLE

Instill in your children a love for reading
by making good books easily available
and by offering appealing alternatives to television and video.

There are many reasons why we might want to steer our children toward good books and away from television and video games. The violent content and sexual overtones in much of what is available are two very good ones; the number of commercials on television is another; the overall low quality of what is offered is yet another.

These are all good reasons; however, none of them is my reason. The reason I want my children to read books instead of watching television is because I want their experience of growing up to be different from mine. During much of my elementary and high school years, I was a reluctant reader who skated through school and wasted a lot of time watching television. As an adult, this has been one of my deepest and most enduring regrets.

I didn't start out that way. Of all the memories of my early childhood, the most vivid are those of my mother reading to me at bedtime. Like all children, I had a number of favorite books, which my mother willingly read to me over and over. I loved it most when she read from *The Illustrated Treasury of Children's Literature*, a big, blue volume filled with nursery rhymes, stories, poems and fairy tales. To this day, when I am still, I can hear the cadence of the song-like rhythm of her voice.

I especially remember being filled with wonder at the magic of books, at how black marks on a page could be silently translated in my mother's mind and read aloud for me to hear. Those words, in turn, formed pictures in my mind, and I could imagine the story. When you think about it, reading is a remarkable thing, and as a young child I had a very clear sense of the marvelousness of the written word.

I was born before *Sesame Street*, so I had to wait until first grade to find out that each letter has its own sound, which when combined with the sounds of other letters forms a word. I had always imagined reading to be a mysterious and possibly arbitrary sort of activity—the letters certainly appeared that way to me—so I was relieved and delighted to learn that there was a clear logic to the process and that with some effort on my part the code could be broken and mastered.

Soon after learning to read, though, around second or third grade, something intervened and I failed to become the eager, enthusiastic reader I might have been. That something, I believe, was television.

As I understand it now, I began to watch a lot of television at exactly the same time I became self-conscious about my creativity and my ability to imagine. This is a sad, though not uncommon, phenomenon. Until the age of seven or eight, children are usually very free and happy about their creativity and artistic abilities. They enthusiastically try new things, and the fact that they don't know how to do something does not occur to them. They simply do it. This open-hearted sensibility reminds me of a quote I once saw on the window of an art store: "I am always doing that which I cannot do, in order that I may learn how to do it." It was attributed to Pablo Picasso (who also said, "It takes a long time to become young").

By the age of eight or nine, however, many children's attitudes undergo a change. They develop a self-consciousness that, in art at least, is revealed in a new unwillingness to take creative risks. They begin comparing their drawings and creations with those of their classmates. They judge (often negatively) their own work. The idea that they don't know how to do something seeps into their awareness.

As I have thought about this, I have realized that this phenomenon coincides with my experience as a child. Whereas my most cherished memories of early childhood include creating forts and spaceships with a blanket and the wooden jungle gym in our backyard; dipping duck feathers into our neighbor's pond and watching, amazed, as they emerged from the water completely dry every time; sipping nectar from honeysuckle blossoms; and, of course, being read to by my mother—my memories after second grade are primarily of watching television. Before school, after school, after dinner (we were never allowed to watch television during a meal), Saturday morning, Sunday afternoon...television became *the* primary way I passed my free time at home. It was as easy as falling into a pit. The shows I watched didn't require any imagination or creativity. They didn't challenge or stimulate. In fact, they didn't require any thought at all. With Dick Van Dyke or Ed Sullivan or Carol Burnett always available, I did not have to be inventive or original, and I rarely had to resort to reading to pass a long afternoon. Secretly, I was relieved since I no longer had to create my own way of passing time.

It was not until I was almost out of high school that I woke up from what I now regard as a "television-induced stupor," and it was not until college that I rediscovered the absolute joy of reading. My deep regret about this loss is my great incentive to do everything I can to create a different experience for my children.

One day I observed my daughter thoroughly absorbed in a mail-order catalog that I apparently had not thrown into the recycling bin fast enough. It was one of those catalogs that sell the kind of cheap plastic toys children seem to love, and I could almost see her mind being taken over with longing for the colorful, sparkly things in there. I recognized the look because I have experienced it myself many times: that driving desire for something that can occupy us for an hour, a day, even a week or longer. For me, the longing was usually for an article of clothing I could not afford. Sometimes I was able to scrape the money together by not buying food for a while (this was when I was single, of course). Yet, whether or not I was able to buy the thing, afterward I always regretted the amount of time I had wasted coveting it.

I've come to realize that children's minds (as well as our own) will not—cannot—remain empty. They will always fill up with something. I want my children's minds to be full of what good books put in there, or what my children put in there themselves through imaginative play—not what television or video games or toy catalogs might provide.

The Reading Principle requires a high level of commitment, because it entails time and effort to offer children alternatives, such as neighborhood walks or boardgames or baking, in addition to a wide and easily accessible supply of books. My husband deserves most of the credit for the time our family spends playing games. He has taught all three of our children (and me) how to play a decent hand of poker. He is always willing to set aside his plans to play a board game or kick a ball around the backyard or play ping pong on the dining room table. My husband is also a master at creating games out of nothing more than a stick and a coin, a pen and paper, or a couple of pancake flippers and a leftover pancake—a talent I deeply admire and sincerely hope my children inherit.

I don't have my husband's competitive gaming spirit, so I am inclined to suggest a walk around the neighborhood when the children need something to do. This is generally a harder sell, and we do it less often than I would like. Still, our kids usually enjoy a walk more than they think they will. And I have noticed that walking generates conversation in a way almost nothing else does. No one is tempted to buy anything, and ideas or concerns surface that I am certain would never have been expressed otherwise. Maybe it has to do with the exercise, or the fact that we are not facing one another, or that the scenery provides a helpful level of distraction, but our walks usually turn out to be wonderful experiences. Somehow walking promotes reconciliation, too, for it seems we all let go of our anger toward one another more quickly than at other times.

For city people like ourselves, regular walks are also one of the few ways to experience our connection with nature and the cosmos. We observe the changing seasons by the lengthening or shortening of the day, the warming or cooling of the temperature, the blossoming or fading of the gardens we pass. We marvel at the clouds and notice the phases of the moon. We try to fathom that—all visual evidence and our vocabulary to the contrary—the sun is not rising, crossing the sky, and setting, but rather the earth is spinning on its tilted axis, moving along its yearly orbit around the sun. One day I posed this vocabulary problem to my children, and I'm hoping one of them will invent two beautiful, new words to replace our woefully inadequate and astronomically incorrect *sunrise* and *sunset*.

A child's mind that has not been filled with video images is just the place where such creative imagining can happen. There is the space for wondering that can form itself into questions, such as the one my then four-year-old daughter once asked me: "Where is the edge of the world?" The remarkable conversation that followed is one I will treasure for the rest of my life.

While my husband and I are committed to spending a good deal of time with our children, I do not feel obligated to find something for them to do every time they are bored. I try to strike a balance, partly because I need time to myself and partly because I know that if our children are constantly being entertained and distracted, whether by us or with a video, they might never reach the level of boredom where their own creativity and imagination can kick in. When they are always entertained, they lose the opportunity to look inward, to become aware of and draw upon their own vast inner resources, to create something out of nothing.

As I continue to reflect on my own childhood I see that while I was glued to the television set there were, in fact, people around me who spent a good deal of time with books. My older sister, for one, loved to read. She generously and enthusiastically passed many of her books along to me—some of which I finished, most of which I did not. I have fond memories of my father sitting in his favorite chair reading Louis L'Amour westerns, while my younger brother lay sprawled on the floor browsing our 1957 *World Book Encyclopedia*. He must have read all twenty volumes during the course of his school years. I do not remember seeing my mother read for herself, but I also do not remember her ever sitting down by herself except to sew or play the piano. With five children and a large house, reading anything but somebody's homework or a bedtime story before 10:00 p.m. must have seemed like a luxury that she could not afford. Once we were all in school, though, and more or less self-reliant, my mother became a volunteer reader for an organization that records books for the blind, and today she is the most well-read person I know.

These recaptured memories of my family life have helped me

realize a very important fact: The only power we parents really have is over our own actions. We can offer, provide, suggest, invite, shape, model and guide, but we cannot force. It is up to each child to choose what he or she is going to do in response.

In other words, growing up without a lot of television or video games does not guarantee that our children will be enthusiastic readers. While I hope very much that our children will experience the delicious pleasure of losing themselves in a book, I can't *make* it happen. When they are grown, the most my husband and I will be able to say is that our children were surrounded by many good books, went for hundreds of walks, played a lot of cards, learned their way around the kitchen, and didn't watch much television. I will be content with that.

9
THE ART
PRINCIPLE

Encourage your children's love for art, in all its forms,
by exposing them to music, painting, theater and dance,
and by providing ample opportunities for creativity
in all areas of their lives.

I included the Art Principle primarily because I wanted to share what I enjoy most with my children, which is going to theater, concerts, and live performances of all sorts. While good intentions are a start in this regard, they are almost never enough. I can easily imagine never getting around to buying tickets for even a fraction of the performances I would like my children to see, mostly because of the expense. Five tickets to almost anything can be quite costly, and somebody always needs a new pair of shoes or the house needs a new furnace or the car needs a new muffler. Making art a priority by including it in this principle makes the decision to write the check that much easier.

However, in order to fully develop this idea for myself, I have had to think more fundamentally about the role of art in my own life. In the process I have both deepened and broadened my thinking about why it is so important that art and creativity be a part of my children's lives.

First, this principle, like many of the others, is a direct response to my childhood experiences. For some reason, I grew up thinking that to be an artist one had to be able to draw. I also believed that creativity was something only artists had. Since I was not able to draw very well, I thought I could never be an artist, and therefore, I suppose for consistency's sake, I also believed I was not creative. I have no idea whether I might have chosen the path of the artist, but the fact is that it was not open to me. It was not within the realm of possibility in my mind.

What I want to do for my children is clear all the paths, open all the doors, and let them know that art is not only drawing but it is *everything*: music, theater, dance, photography, writing, cooking, gardening, conversation—anything, in fact, that is accomplished with truth and beauty in mind. I want them to know that, in short, art *is* life and life *is* art.

Second, as I mentioned, I have a strong desire to share my love for live performance. The reason I find live performance so compelling is that when I observe someone using his or her talent and imagination in an act of conscious creation I feel I can practically touch that person's joyful soul. There is something about using one's whole body to create and perform that is profoundly moving to me. At those times I understand most clearly that we were made to create and are most in tune with God when we are consciously doing so. It is a different feeling that I have from watching a movie, which can be shot and re-shot and edited until each scene is perfect, not to mention viewed over and over again. For me, much of the value of live performance lies in its uniqueness and imperfection. It is literally a once-in-a-lifetime event, never to be repeated in exactly the same way again. Whether I am listening to an orchestra or watching a street performer, I am acutely aware of the universal singularity of this moment in time. In the midst of our culture of abundance, I want my children to experience rarity.

Third, I want to be intentional about making sure that my children are exposed regularly to beauty and the higher ideals that beauty, above all else, is able to convey. This is critical because what children see by default contains very little beauty. Television, movies and advertising, in particular, while at times visually captivating, are only fast food for the eyes, incapable of essential nourishment for the soul.

Beauty, on the other hand, inspires a different response. Elaine Scarry, in her book *On Beauty and Being Just*, observes that when we see something beautiful, we are moved to respond in some way. We either want to keep the beautiful thing in our sight for as long as possible, as a bird in our binoculars, or we want to replicate it by drawing it or photographing it or writing about it. Even simply describing the beautiful thing to someone else is a form of replication. Scarry's notion confirms for me that we were made for beauty. We notice it. We respond to it. We want to re-create it, and in so doing, we create it anew. My hope is that by seeing original art and live performances my children will be inspired to create things for themselves.

It has taken the kids and me some time to find the right medium. It never worked simply to sit down with them and draw. Misgivings about my own drawing abilities were a factor, as was figuring out exactly what to draw. Whenever my husband (who draws extremely well) sat down with us, all we wanted to do was watch him.

Eventually, I was forced to acknowledge that none of us were at the "art for art's sake" stage. However, I did notice that there was considerably more interest and enthusiasm if the proposed art project had a function. Thus, we began our creative endeavors by decorating Christmas cookies, coloring Easter eggs, cutting snowflakes and folding origami cranes. Along the way we expanded our operations to include making birthday cards, thank-you notes, miscellaneous greeting cards, and paper sculptures of all sorts. It turns out that these simple, repetitive activities offered the very experience I was looking for without exactly knowing it. Because we make so many cards or cookies at a time, we don't fret over the design of each one. Our joy lies in getting lost in the process, in experiencing the flow, not in the outcome of a single creation.

More recently, I have set my sights miles above and beyond the art that is accomplished at our dining room table. My eyes were raised to this lofty height after my children and I attended a local production of C. S. Lewis' *The Silver Chair*. I was so impressed with the creativity that went into the retelling of this marvelous story that for days afterward I thought about little else. I vividly imagined the conversations, collaboration and cooperation that would have been required to create the simple but highly evocative set, the atmospheric lighting, and the terrifically imaginative costumes. I thought about how the whole thing was accomplished with limited time, space and budget—and above all without the special effects upon which movies routinely rely. It seemed to me that the production of this play was an act of pure creation of the highest sort, joyful and life-giving for all who were involved. A dream was born in me.

I have since then quietly and surreptitiously encouraged my children to become involved in theater productions wherever and whenever possible. (I have learned that covert operations are best when trying to get my children to be interested in something I am interested in. If they feel they are being pushed, if they feel *at all* that I am telling them what to do, they run the other way as fast as they can.)

At this point I must admit I have another motive for getting involved in theater besides encouraging my children's creativity. It has been my experience that I get blamed for a lot of the stuff that goes wrong in our household. I suppose this is because parents, in the eyes of children, are tremendously powerful people. We seem to know just about everything, we have the most money, we can reach high places, and we don't have to ask for our allowance. So, when the desired shirt is not clean, or someone cannot find a shoe, or we are out of peanut butter, parents seem to be the natural target for blame. Aren't we running the show? Maybe this is a normal developmental stage, but I resist it strenuously. In my opinion, children cannot start accepting responsibility for their part in the "family play" soon enough.

Theater offers invaluable life lessons, starting with the realization that each performance is different. In one, someone might forget a line (read: we are out of peanut butter), or some prop isn't where it's supposed to be (read: the dirty shirt is not in the laundry basket), or something goes wrong behind stage that must be fixed in a hurry or improvised (read: we all overslept). This is life. Sometimes we do things right, sometimes not. In a play, the cooperation of everyone is assumed. Everyone works hard to be prepared, but things go wrong. Mistakes are made. In theater you don't stop everything in the middle of the show to examine the problem or lay blame for the mistake. The show goes on, and only afterward, in the context of the whole play (read: family meeting), are the mistakes noted and, hopefully, learned from. The spirit of enthusiastic cooperation and conscious creation is what I am after—the compassion and understanding that comes from feeling that we are all in this together, that everyone is doing his or her part, that sometimes we fail but we all have a stake in the outcome.

I know—it's a dream.

For a long time nothing happened, because I still didn't understand that it was just that: *my* dream. I found myself wishing everyone else would be enthusiastically cooperative, and then I would be too. With time, however, I came to accept responsibility for realizing my dream. I now know that I need to be the one who demonstrates the ideals of cooperation and conscious creation. Being mindful of my leading role helps me (sometimes) to remember to smile when I want to yell, to be enthusiastic when I am grumpy, to say nothing when I want to blame.

Beyond the artistic, hands-on kind of creativity, there is an even wider world of intellectual creativity, the kind that uses imagery, metaphor and dialogue to reveal assumptions, solve problems, and promote understanding. This is another area that I want to help my children—as well as myself and my husband—develop.

As usual, I take my inspiration where I find it. In this instance it is a wonderfully wise children's story by James Thurber called *Many Moons*. It is about a princess who falls ill from a "surfeit of raspberry tarts." She declares she will not become well unless her father gives her the moon. The king's advisors, who had heretofore always been able to get for him anything he wanted—including sand from the sandman, angels' feathers, and unicorns' horns—are not able to figure out how to get the moon. In fact, they do not even agree on how big the moon is, how far away it might be, or even what it is made of. The king's jester observes, "They are all wise men, and so they must all be right. If they are all right, then the moon must be just as large and as far away as each person thinks it is. The thing to do is find out how big the Princess Lenore thinks it is, and how far away." In the end it is the princess herself who provides the answers that allow the jester to give her the moon.

What I try to remember from this beautiful story is that we parents are inclined to hand conclusions to our children rather than make it possible for them to find their own solutions and discover their own truths. We do this, I think, because we *like* our conclusions—or at least we are invested in them. They are like family heirlooms that have been handed down for generations. We had to live with these conclusions, why shouldn't our children?

I hope that by keeping the door to creativity open, I will avoid passing on to my children false notions about what is possible and what is impossible, what is fitting and proper and what is not, what can and cannot be done. I want to be a model of openness, possibility and creativity. I want consciously to avoid laying my preconceived notions and rigid assumptions onto my children. Instead, I want to give them the freedom to discover and reveal their own truths, just as the jester did for the princess.

My incentive is that this approach works beautifully! When I manage to remember that this is what I want to do, the solutions that my children discover are far more imaginative and interesting than anything I might have thought of. And if their solution involves a restriction of some kind, such as time or money, my children are usually happy to deal with it because *they thought of it in the first place.*

Ultimately, when our children come of age, I hope they will not be satisfied working at some mindless job in a stifling atmosphere but will insist on doing work that demands imagination and creativity. Wouldn't it be wonderful if our children would refuse to work in cramped cubicles for huge multinational corporations? Then we could create the kind of economy described by E. F. Schumacher in his book *Small is Beautiful*:

> The type of work which modern technology is most successful in reducing or even eliminating is skillful, productive work of human hands, in touch with real materials of one kind or another. In an advanced industrial society, such work has become exceedingly rare, and to make a decent living by doing such work has become virtually impossible. A great part of the modern neurosis may be due to this very fact: for the human being, defined by Thomas Aquinas as a being with brains and hands, enjoys nothing more than to be creatively, usefully, productively engaged with both his hands and his brains.

I have no idea what my children will do when they grow up, but I hope that their early exposure to art in all its forms ensures that they will embrace creativity as essential to their existence here on earth and as a way to commune with God. For I believe conscious creativity is nothing less than God working through us. Teilhard de Chardin in *Hymn of the Universe* described this dynamic beautifully:

> God, at his most vitally active and most incarnate, is not remote from us, wholly apart from the sphere of the tangible; on the contrary, at every moment he awaits us in the activity, the work to be done, which every moment brings. He is, in a sense, at the point of my pen, my pick, my paint-brush, my needle—and my heart and my thought. It is by carrying to its natural completion the stroke, the line, the stitch I am working on that I shall lay hold of that ultimate end towards which my will at its deepest level tends.

My highest hope is that my children will not grow up thinking art is only for artists and creativity somehow takes place only in an art studio or a theater. I hope they understand that creativity is intrinsic to our nature. Human beings cannot *not* create. Creativity is not something that only artists do, it is something that we all do every day, whether we are aware of it or not. I want my children to know that art is an integral part of a *lived* life, a life that is rich and full in the highest meaning of the term.

If my children grow up knowing through their lived experience the truth of this reality, if they approach their own creativity with the reverence and wonder and awe that it deserves, I will have realized my dream.

10
THE FORGIVENESS
PRINCIPLE

*Model humility for your children
by saying you are sorry
and asking for forgiveness.*

When I decided to include the Forgiveness Principle, it was partly because I was bugged by my children's unwillingness to accept responsibility for their behavior and partly because I wanted to have one thing on this list that I do naturally and well. I had learned from my father how to identify my contribution to a conflict, admit it, and apologize. I'm pretty good at that by now, and for a long time I thought apologizing was all there was to forgiveness. I have since learned otherwise.

One afternoon I did not pick up my children after school because my youngest child was taking a nap, and I did not want to wake her. (We live close enough to our school that the older two can walk home without me.) My daughter was furious. She had missed the chance to play at her friend's house because I was not there to give my permission. She was frustrated and bored and unwilling to let it go. After saying "I'm sorry!" for the tenth time, I leaned into her face and said, "I am sorry! Will you forgive me?" It seems like a simple thing to say, but it changed the whole dynamic of our argument. As long as I kept saying, "I'm sorry," no action or change was required on her part. However, as soon as I engaged my daughter by asking for forgiveness, she relented. She said yes, she would forgive me, and the confrontation, which had been going on for some time, ended.

When I reflected on what happened, I realized I had always thought that saying "I'm sorry" was the same as asking for forgiveness. The confrontation with my daughter showed me the difference. Reconciliation requires that one person is sorry *and* that the other forgives. I had been so concerned about showing my children how to say the "I'm sorry" part that I had forgotten the other half of the equation, the "Will you forgive me?" part.

Asking for forgiveness turned out to be a painless phrase to tack onto my apology. It was a simple tag line that helped to end a confrontation quickly, and for a short time I was able to continue thinking of the Forgiveness Principle as the "easy" one. This illusion reminds me of a story my daughter once wrote that ended, "And they lived happily ever after until the next day." Because it took about that long for my children to catch on. Now, when I am angry with one of them, they will quickly say, "I'm sorry! Will you forgive me?"

Sometimes the hardest thing to do is to walk through a door you have opened yourself. Asking for forgiveness is one thing; bestowing forgiveness is something else altogether. Full and true reconciliation, it turns out, is a hard business for me. When I am offended, I like to remain offended, at least for what seems like a decent period of time. I think I have earned it somehow, and I do not like to give it up too soon. Sometimes, I am sorry to admit, it feels too difficult to forgive because I am tired or grumpy or because there have been one too many offenses that day. Those are the times when the words "Okay, I forgive you" literally stick in my throat and, try as I might, I cannot make myself say them. Too bad for me, though, because then the harsh words play over and over again in my mind, while my child has completely forgotten about our argument and happily gone on to something else.

Other days, I am able to reach all the way down through my resentment and anger and fear, and bring the words "I forgive you" up to my lips. At those times, even if I do not feel it beforehand, an extraordinary transformation takes place and I experience a feeling of forgiveness. Saying the words somehow causes the feeling. It is always remarkable, always surprising. I have no idea how or why it works, but I do think it is one of the most important things we can ever learn how to do.

Jesus certainly thought so. His most pointed words on this subject are recorded thus: "If you forgive the sins of any, they are forgiven them; if you retain the sins of any, they are retained" (John 20:23). I take this to mean that when we forgive someone, that person is forgiven, but when we do not, he or she is not. Jesus might well have added, "But then *you* are the one who is stuck."

In my clumsy attempts to understand and develop my own capacity for forgiveness and reconciliation, I have stumbled upon an important truth: Events, in and of themselves, are neutral. It is the individual, through his or her interpretation, who decides whether events are positive or negative, whether they honor or offend, whether they are a blessing or a curse.

I became consciously aware of this through an exercise described in a book called *Sleeping with Bread* by Dennis Linn, Sheila Fabricant Linn and Matthew Linn. Our family gathers around the dinner table and each person answers two questions: "For what am I most grateful?" and "For what am I least grateful?" The purpose of this "examen," based on the spiritual exercises of St. Ignatius, is to notice and identify those experiences that are life-giving and those that are life-draining. The resulting self-awareness alone makes the examen worthwhile.

However, when our family does this simple exercise, we derive at least three additional benefits. The first is that each of us gets a glimpse of what happened that day to the others. This is particularly helpful as our children get older and spend more time away from home. Second, we are developing the habit of genuine gratitude. By taking a few moments to think about our response, we inevitably notice the myriad things for which we are grateful that might otherwise have been forgotten or overlooked. We have found that often it is hard to pick just one to share, and it is not uncommon that one of us cannot think of anything for which we are least grateful. Finally, it sometimes turns out that what one person is most grateful for is the very thing for which another person is least grateful.

When this happens, all of us are reminded that daily happenings are simply part of "what is," and that it is *our response* that gives them meaning. This, in turn, confirms that each of us has a different perspective and affirms that one single view, response or reaction is not the only possibility. This realization can lead to other discoveries. Once we acknowledge that our way is not the only way, we become capable of noticing that each of us has an inner life that while vividly real to ourselves is nevertheless invisible to others. It opens a window to understanding that what really makes us who we are—our thoughts, feelings, emotions, hopes, fears, dreams, likes and dislikes—is invisible.

As E. F. Schumacher notes in *A Guide for the Perplexed*, "We tend to see ourselves primarily in the light of our intentions, which are invisible to others, while we see others mainly in the light of their actions, which are visible to us.... [This creates] a situation in which misunderstanding and injustice are the order of the day."

Developing our capacity for compassion and forgiveness goes hand-in-hand with increasing consciousness of our inner life, otherwise known as *self-awareness*. When I am self-aware, I am obliged to admit when I have been selfish, rude, unkind, careless, irresponsible—or at least not done what I said I would do. How can I get angry or delay forgiving my child for the same thing? Jesus put it this way:

> "Why do you see the speck in your neighbor's eye, but do not notice the log in your own eye? Or how can you say to your neighbor, 'Friend, let me take out the speck in your eye,' when you yourself do not see the log in your own eye? You hypocrite, first take the log out of your own eye, and then you will see clearly to take the speck out of your neighbor's eye." (Luke 6:41-42)

Children, I have observed, are not the ones who need to learn how to forgive. They are not very good at saying they are sorry, but they are happy to forgive. I, on the other hand, have a lot of work to do in this area. Fortunately, my children will no doubt provide me with many opportunities to practice forgiveness in the days and years to come. My hope is that if my husband and I work on our part—modeling humility and practicing self-awareness—our children will not forget what they now know intuitively: that forgiveness is freedom and holding onto grudges is not.

If that happens, we all might live happily ever after, far beyond the next day.

11
The "Yes" Principle

Say yes to your children as often as possible.

Of all the principles in this book, the "Yes" Principle is the most elusive to define. The "say yes" part is clear enough; it's the "as often as possible" part that makes it seem arbitrary and ambiguous. My intention is not, as my children might hope, to declare that parents should say yes to as many requests as possible, no matter how expensive or inappropriate. It is rather to convey an attitude of openness and a willingness to listen without judgment. It is a reminder to pause before responding; to look beyond the mess that any given proposition is sure to cause; and to consider the possibilities for creativity, learning, and just plain fun that often lie hidden within a request.

It is important to note at the outset that this principle rarely applies to *buying* things (which constitutes the vast majority of children's requests), but rather to *doing* things. It is a prompt to say yes to an experience, not to another toy or pair of shoes or whatever the desire of the moment is. It means saying yes to time with our children; yes to helping them make something for which they have an idea; yes to giving them the freedom to experiment on their own; yes to expressing themselves.

At the same time, I think of the "as often as possible" part as the escape clause. It applies the brakes and provides the caution that helps to distinguish between what is a reasonable—even if inconvenient—request and what is unhealthy, unsafe or inappropriate. The "Yes" Principle and the Structure Principle work together to create a two-part system that balances the anarchical tendencies in the one and the controlling tendencies in the other. In other words, saying yes counters the control that having too much structure might impose, and having structure counters the chaos that saying yes all the time might produce.

The seeds of the "Yes" Principle were planted when our first child was about two years old. His imagination and ability to articulate what he was imagining were beginning to coincide, and he could communicate what he wanted to do with a fair amount of accuracy. As I discovered, and as any parent no doubt knows, there are few things more fun and interesting than spending time with young children while they explore the world. The freedom, creativity, and wondering of children produce pure magic. I loved watching my son. Anything he could imagine and express, I was willing to help him accomplish.

As time went on, however, I noticed that my enthusiasm was waning considerably. Maybe it was my longing for a clean, orderly house again, but more and more often I wanted to say no to his projects, which seemed mostly to involve either using large amounts of cardboard, aluminum foil and tape, or cooking with messy ingredients, such as lots and lots of flour. I learned that there are few things as time consuming as cleaning up spilled flour (unless it's cleaning up spilled flour and water, otherwise known as glue).

My increasing resistance bothered me, so before responding I tried to ask myself, "Am I opposed to this idea because it's unhealthy or dangerous, or because I just don't want the mess that it's sure to cause?" If it were the latter, I would try to say yes in spite of the inconvenience. I was always glad when I did.

With the arrival of our second child, things changed dramatically. A little less freedom and a lot more order were what I thought I needed to get through the day. Looking back, the line that divided what was important and what was not—so clear a few months earlier—disappeared with startling swiftness. Once in a while I would catch myself and think, "Why do I care that she wears black socks with her jelly sandals?" and back off for a day or so. But it never lasted very long. I learned the hard way that once you start trying to control your children it is very difficult to give it up—even when you notice, as you surely must, that it does not work.

At one point during this extended tug of war with myself, I saw a movie called *Fly Away Home*. It is about a young girl named Amy who came to live with her father in rural Canada after the death of her mother. As a parent, I of course identified with the father. Except I noticed that the father said yes to his daughter when I would have said no. Moreover, I realized that his consistent "yes" moved the story along; it, in fact, made the whole adventure possible.

One morning Amy found an abandoned nest of goose eggs and brought them into the barn to keep them warm. But soon the baby geese were in the house—on the kitchen table, on the couch, and in the bathroom. At this point, I am certain I would have said no. But this father said yes. A ranger arrived, intending to clip their wings so the geese could not fly. If I had been talked into keeping the geese, I surely would have bowed to the ranger's authority and allowed their wings to be clipped. The father did not. Then the geese needed to fly south for the winter. If I had had the courage to oppose the ranger's authority (and that is a very big if), at this point, I surely would have said, "Sorry! That's impossible! We cannot fly these geese south for the winter."

The father once again said yes and proceeded to build a small flying machine that Amy could pilot herself and that the motherless geese would follow. The final scene shows Amy flying over the South Carolina coast with the geese following her, with Mary Chapin Carpenter singing "10,000 Miles" in the background. The beauty of that scenery and music chokes me up every time.

This movie made such an impression on me that I was inspired once again to try to say yes to my children's requests. Most importantly, it provided me with a critical question to ask myself when considering a request: "Will this move the story forward?" Ice cream at 5:00 p.m. won't; neither will a PG-13 movie for a ten year old, or one more stuffed animal, no matter how soft and adorable it is. On the other hand, leftover birthday cake for breakfast will move the story forward (as evidenced by my own fond memories of this very thing); so will using every pillow and blanket in the house to build a fort in the living room; or letting a gaggle of children loose in the kitchen with a cookbook, a few ingredients, and food coloring.

As the idea of saying yes as often as possible became more and more integrated into my daily thinking, I became aware of other classic "yes" stories. Two Bible stories in particular had a significant impact on the development of this principle: "The Annunciation" and "The Prodigal Son."

Mary's response to the angel Gabriel is probably the most famous "yes" of all time: "Let it be with me according to your word" (Luke 1:38). And although I've always thought that it would be easier to say yes to an angel than to a sixteen year old wanting to drive your car for the first time, Mary's response nevertheless is a powerful and inspiring example of blind faith and courage. She did not really have any idea what she was saying yes to, and neither do we most of the time. Her "yes" was really a "yes" to *whatever* life has to offer. So can ours be.

One of the most beautiful and moving hymns I've ever heard is inspired, at least in part, by Mary's response to Gabriel. It is called "Servant Song" by Donna Marie McGargill, and the last lines of each verse are, "*I am your song…. Sing your songs in me…. Let it be done to me.*" Mary's story is a reminder that to say yes is to allow God to sing in us—and that a child with a crazy idea could be an angel in disguise.

In the other Bible story, "The Prodigal Son," it is also the father's unconditional "yes" that makes the story possible. Without it, the son could not have left his family in the first place, let alone have had the money to support himself and his extravagant lifestyle. And if he hadn't left, there would have been no opportunity to learn about himself and no reason for the father to demonstrate his unconditional love upon the son's return.

In addition to the father's "yes," there are at least two additional truths in this story that have helped me shape the ideas underlying the "Yes" Principle: By saying yes, we give our children the freedom to become who they are; and each unconditional "yes" gives our children the freedom to make mistakes. I think these are two of the greatest gifts a parent can give a child.

We all yearn to become who we are. That is one of the reasons we are here. In order to become who we are, we have to try many different paths and ways of being. Young children cannot do this if they hear "no" more often than "yes." On the other hand, when children frequently hear "yes" to their ideas, plans and dreams, they gain confidence in their decisions, their abilities, their creativity, themselves.

An unconditional "yes" means that we do not say "I told you so" when our child's decision turns out to be what we might judge to be a bad one. All we have to do is look at our own lives to know that mistakes, or what seemed like wrong turns or detours at the time, can contain valuable information that could not have been acquired in any other way. For one thing, mistakes make clear, or help us appreciate, what we have done that is right. For another, they provide a corrective in direction and focus, which brings us that much closer to what we really want.

A wise aunt put it to me this way when I couldn't decide where or what to study in college: "It is as important to find out what you *don't* like as it is to find out what you *do* like. Nothing is a waste of time." I was relieved and reassured by her comment, and since then I have felt free to study and work in a variety of different fields. I am grateful to her and my parents (who never said, "I told you so") because I have learned something worthwhile from every experience. I want nothing less for my own children.

As children get older, the kinds of requests and proposals they present will necessarily change. Many requests will be easy to say yes to: putting up a tent in the backyard for a weekend, running a backyard summer camp, cleaning out a corner of the basement or the attic for a special space. And, inevitably, many will not: a hairstyle we can't stand, clothing we would never wear but otherwise have no real objection to, certain friends we would never choose for them.

My children would be the first to volunteer their opinion that I do not say yes as much as they would like. They are quick to quote this principle—which is apparently the only one they know by heart—when I say no to watching a movie on a school night or sitting in the front seat of our car before they are thirteen. Still, they know that I am inclined to say yes, that I want to say yes, and that I will say yes if the request is safe, reasonably healthy (or at least not completely unhealthy), and age appropriate.

Ultimately, I hope by growing up hearing "yes" to their ideas, to what's possible, to who they are, that my children will not be afraid to experiment; to make mistakes; to try, learn and grow. I hope they will be conscious creators, artists in the broadest sense of the term, with life itself as their medium. I hope through them God will sing full-throated a song of beauty and grace never heard before.

12
THE HUMOR
PRINCIPLE

Do all of the above with a sense of humor.

Although I included this final principle because I know that a sense of humor is important, I never really thought that I would be able to live up to it. If you have read this far, you may have noticed that I am more of a reflective person, not exactly a wellspring of humorous stories and anecdotes. I am not very good at telling a joke, either, as anyone who knows me will attest.

As I have reflected on what the Humor Principle really means, though, I have realized that to have a sense of humor as a parent does not mean being able to tell a joke. I do not have to be able to think of snappy one-liners or quick comebacks to qualify as someone who lives with amusement. I do, however, have to be able to step outside of the daily dramas and dilemmas that are an integral part of parenting and develop a perspective that includes humor. I can learn to do that!

It is always easier to see the humor in the faults and foibles of others, so that is not a bad place to begin. The daughter of a friend of mine comes to mind. Over the years, under many circumstances, I have never once seen her do as her mother asked, even after several even-tempered requests. Invariably, the daughter completely ignores her mother who, incidentally, handles the rejection very well. Now, I think this is very funny. Why? Because she is not my child! She is not my child, so my self-esteem is not wrapped up in how she behaves. She is not my child, so I can see her for what she is—an imperfect, unfinished human; a work in progress, as we all are. I can appreciate her determination to be autonomous because I know this is what all children strive to become—and rightly so.

For me to see humor in the same dynamic with my own children is a great gift. It helps me remember that life as a parent can be very amusing when we can step outside of the drama and see ourselves the way we see others: with detachment, compassion and amusement.

I realize this, but I forget it more often than I would like. When I lose my sense of humor, however, what I am really doing is turning over my personal power to another person. If I am anything other than neutral and amused when my child is having a tantrum, I am in *her* power. She is controlling me. She is the one directing the show, and I am merely an actor in her production. At those times, I remind myself of Napoleon the dog in Walt Disney's *The Aristocats,* who keeps insisting, "Ah'm the Leader!" even though his sidekick Lafayette is already ten steps ahead.

To be amused is to decide to place oneself outside the influence of other people. I have noticed to my great delight that my children, or anyone else for that matter, have no power over me when I am amused. It doesn't mean that I don't care about them; it does mean that I can decide not to be pulled into the *sturm und drang* of their problems and dilemmas.

So how do we choose humor as a response on a regular basis? My experience is that the first step is awareness. I began by noticing that, unlike my husband, I almost never chose to be amused at my children's behavior. Next, I asked myself two questions: "What am I choosing instead of amusement?" and "Why am I choosing it?"

My answer to the first question is that I usually choose to be offended when my children say what I would never say, or do what I never remember doing as a child. My answer to the second question is a bit more complicated. Why do I choose to be offended? For a fair number of reasons, it seems, the first having to do with my expectations about how children behave toward their parents (which I am continually having to set aside) and the second having to do with habit. My response is automatic and unthinking, and in that sense it is an addiction. Scientists are discovering that when we respond to a given situation in a particular way, then choose to do that many times over, our bodies become addicted to the chemicals that are created from that response. Over time it becomes more difficult to choose any other way, or even to imagine what another response might be.

Finally, I've noticed that to be offended creates drama, and drama is exciting. Whether our own or other people's, drama creates a sense of urgency and importance that can become the only way we really feel alive. It might be the only way we think we can communicate with others or that others feel they can communicate with us. Unfortunately, drama is not very much fun.

Only after becoming aware that we do not choose amusement on a regular basis, and why, can we decide to make a change. There are probably a great number of approaches to this sort of transformation; here are two that I use. I learned once in a meditation class that the center of our head is the "seat," as it were, of our neutrality and amusement. When our attention is resting there, we can access this state of mind quite easily. To find the center of your head, imagine a line going from just above one ear through your head to the other ear. Next, imagine a line going from the middle of your forehead to the back of your head. The place where these two lines intersect is the center of your head. Try focusing your attention there. If you can keep your attention in the center of your head for more than a few seconds—which takes a lot of practice—you will find that you can remain neutral and amused even while your child has a tantrum in front of ten people at the grocery store.

The other thing to do is simply smile when your child says what you would never have dreamed of saying to your parents. Probably for the same mysterious reasons that saying "I forgive you" causes forgiveness, the act of smiling creates amusement. My unscientific theory on this phenomenon is that every muscle in our body stores emotion and that when we change the muscle (for example, by un-furrowing our brow and smiling), we change the emotion. All I really know is that it works for me.

These two techniques, along with my unfolding understanding of my personal power to choose a response, have expanded my capacity for amusement to a degree I could not have imagined just a short time ago. I have high hopes that, with a lot of patience and practice, I really will be able to *Do all of the above with a sense of humor.*

Sometimes there's really nothing else for a parent to do.

POSTLUDE

Thank you for reading this book. If we are both lucky, you have learned something that is helpful to you in your challenging role as a parent.

However, I realize that not all of these principles will resonate with you. This book is really an invitation to look at your own life, to identify what values are important to you to pass along to your children, to decide what kind of environment you want to create in your family, and to parent consciously and intentionally.

I recommend that you begin, as I did, by making your own list of "unbreakable (except when necessary) principles of parenting." What you write down on the next two pages as a first draft will tell you a great deal about what you think is important, where your energies lie, and what your focus is. Live with the list for a while, see what you notice, then make any changes you think are necessary. One thing I am certain you will realize is how well you are doing as a parent already. The thought that kept returning to my mind as I wrote my list and then this book is, "I guess I'm not such a hopeless parent after all!"

My Personal Parenting Principles

1. _____

_____

_____

2. _____

_____

_____

3. _____

_____

_____

4. _____

_____

_____

5. _____

_____

_____

6. _____

_____

_____

7. _____

_____

_____

8. _____

_____

_____

9. _____

_____

_____

10. _____

_____

_____

11. _____

_____

_____

12. _____

_____

_____

REFERENCES

Cameron, Julia. *The Artist's Way*. New York: Jeremy P. Tarcher/Putnam, 1992.

Carson, Rachel. *The Sense of Wonder*. New York: HarperCollins, 1998.

Lewis, C. S., *The Silver Chair*. New York: HarperCollins, 1953.

Linn, Dennis; Sheila Fabricant Linn and Matthew Linn. *Sleeping with Bread*. Mahwah, NJ: Paulist Press, 1995.

Martignoni, Margaret E. *The Illustrated Treasury of Children's Literature*. New York: Grosset and Dunlap, 1955.

Ryan, M. J., ed. *A Grateful Heart: Daily Blessings for the Evening Meal from Buddha to the Beatles*. Berkeley: Conari Press, 1994.

Scarry, Elaine. *On Beauty and Being Just*. Princeton: Princeton University Press, 1999.

Schumacher, E. F. *Small is Beautiful*. New York: Harper & Row, 1973.

———. *A Guide for the Perplexed*. New York: Harper & Row, 1977.

Schut, Michael, ed. *Food & Faith*. Denver: Living the Good News, 2002.

———. *Simpler Living, Compassionate Life: A Christian Perspective*. Denver: Living the Good News, 1999.

Teilhard de Chardin, Pierre. *Hymn of the Universe*. New York: Harper Torchbooks, 1969.

Thurber, James. *Many Moons*. New York: Harcourt Brace Jovanovich Inc., 1943.

ADDITIONAL READING

Berry, Wendell. *Life is a Miracle*. Washington, D.C.: Counterpoint, 2000.

Bohm, David and Peat, F. David. *Science, Order, and Creativity*. New York: Bantam Books, 1987.

Brussat, Frederic and Mary Ann. *Spiritual Literacy: Reading the Sacred in Everyday Life*. New York: Scribner, 1996.

Csikszentmihalyi, Mihaly. *Finding Flow*. New York: Basic Books, 1997.

Sanford, John A. *The Kingdom Within, Revised Edition*. New York: HarperCollins, 1987.

ACKNOWLEDGMENTS

It's only when you sit down to write the acknowledgments for a book that you realize just how many people contributed to what you previously thought of as *your* book. I would like to mention a few of them:

Thank you to my colleagues in the rectory of St. Gertrude Parish, Father Bill Kenneally and Peter Buttitta, for believing I had something to say before I believed it myself.

Thank you to my artist friend Deborah Boardman for introducing me to *The Artist's Way*. I am certain my book would not have been started or finished otherwise.

Thank you to my good friend Bob Backis for giving me the idea and the courage to write the initial book proposal.

Thank you to Greg Pierce at ACTA Publications for taking a chance on an unknown writer.

Thank you to my wonderful mother, Ann McCloskey Lang, for being my model and guide, and for making sure that my English is correct.

Thank you to my editor, Marcia Broucek, for taking my manuscript and sculpting it into the good book that you are holding in your hands.

And finally, thank you to my husband, Ed, and my children, Ryan, Ellie and Gina, for their constant inspiration.